Customs Around the World

HOLIDAYS
Around the World

by Wil Mara

PEBBLE
a capstone imprint

Pebble Explore is published by Pebble, an imprint of Capstone.
1710 Roe Crest Drive
North Mankato, Minnesota 56003
www.capstonepub.com

Library of Congress Cataloging-in-Publication Data
Names: Mara, Wil, author. | Pebble (Firm)
Title: Holidays around the world / by Wil Mara.
Description: North Mankato, MN : Pebble, 2020. | Series: Customs around the world | Includes webography. | Audience: Ages 7-8 years | Audience: Grades 2-3 | Summary: "Get ready to celebrate! People around the world look forward to different holidays and honor them with special traditions. Learn about the many types of holidays and how they're celebrated in this engaging series that develops kids' understanding of our diverse global community and their place in it"-- Provided by publisher.
Identifiers: LCCN 2020000942 (print) | LCCN 2020000943 (ebook) | ISBN 9781977123695 (Hardcover) | ISBN 9781977126696 (Paperback) | ISBN 9781977124067 (Adobe PDF)
Subjects: LCSH: Holidays--Juvenile literature. | Festivals--Juvenile literature.
Classification: LCC GT3933 .M33 2020 (print) | LCC GT3933 (ebook) | DDC 394.26--dc23LC record available at https://lccn.loc.gov/2020000942LC ebook record available at https://lccn.loc.gov/2020000943

Image Credits
Alamy: Christian Mueringer, 7; Getty Images: John S Lander/Contributor, 23; iStockphoto: SeanShot, 6, shapecharge, 5, tovfia, 8; Newscom: Xinhua News Agency/Shao Haijun, 26; Shutterstock: Asianet-Pakistan, 11, Auribe, Cover, blueeyes, 9, DreamSlamStudio, 21, GTS Productions, 24, hbpro, 17, JG ARIF WIBOWO, 27, Jim Barber, 16, Kobby Dagan, 22, Sheila Fitzgerald, 20, Snehal Jeevan Pailkar, 12, Stephen Barnes, 25, StockImageFactory.com, 13, 28, View Apart, 4, Yeongsik Im, 15, zhao jiankang, 1, 19

Design Elements
Capstone; Shutterstock: Stawek (map), VLADGRIN

Editorial Credits
Editor: Abby Huff; Designer: Julie Peters; Media Researcher: Jo Miller; Production Specialist: Spencer Rosio

Consultant Credits
Bryan K. Miller, PhD
Research Affiliate of Museum of Anthropological Archaeology
University of Michigan

All internet sites appearing in back matter were available and accurate when this book was sent to press.

TABLE OF CONTENTS

Let's Celebrate! 4

Religious Holidays 6

Marking the New Year 16

Celebrate Your Country 20

Holidays That Help
Us Remember 22

Harvest Time 26

Map 29

Glossary 30

Read More 31

Internet Sites.............. 31

Index 32

Words in **bold** are in the glossary.

LET'S CELEBRATE!

What do you think of when you hear the word *holiday*? Do you think of good food? Spending time with family and friends? No school? These are all great holiday things!

Some holidays have to do with religion. Others help us remember important days in history. There are many holiday **customs** around the world. Just like you, people **celebrate** in special ways!

RELIGIOUS HOLIDAYS

A religion is a set of beliefs people follow. Many holidays mark an important event in a religion.

Christians look forward to Christmas. It remembers the birth of Jesus. Many celebrate on December 25. Families go to church. They give each other gifts.

A family sets up a Nativity scene.

A Christmas tree in Germany

Some people in Italy set up Nativity scenes. These show baby Jesus and his parents. In Germany and other places, trees are often brought into homes. People cover them in bright lights.

Jewish people mark the new year with Rosh Hashanah. In Israel, it is usually celebrated in September for two days. Jewish people get together to pray. A ram's horn is blown. It reminds people to think about mistakes they have made. Then they think about how they can become better.

The ram's horn is called a shofar.

Apples with honey are eaten during Rosh Hashanah.

Later, many families eat apple slices dipped in honey. It means they will have a sweet year!

One month every year, **Muslims** around the world fast. They don't eat during the day. This holiday is called Ramadan. It's a time to pray and be kind.

People celebrate the end of fasting with another holiday. It's Eid al-Fitr. In Pakistan and other places, people gather to pray in the morning. After, they hug and say, "Blessed Eid!" Then family and friends visit each other. They eat lots of good food. Adults give children gifts of money.

People in Pakistan say, "Blessed Eid!"

Hindus have fun during Diwali. This holiday is usually in October or November. It lasts for five days. Diwali celebrates the power of good over evil.

Lighting lamps for Diwali

Patterns made of flowers or colored sand are called *rangoli.*

In India, lights and oil lamps fill the streets. They light up homes too. People also make pretty patterns on the ground with flowers or colored sand. They believe these **decorations** will lead a goddess into their home. She will bring happiness to the whole family.

Buddhists celebrate Buddha's birthday. It is a time to remember the life of the Buddha. It is often in May or April.

During the holiday, many people bring food and flowers to their local **temple**. In South Korea and other places, they pour water over statues of Buddha. It's a way to show thanks for his teachings. The water also reminds people to get rid of bad actions and thoughts.

A child in South Korea pours water on a Buddha statue.

MARKING THE NEW YEAR

One year ends. A new one begins! Millions of people around the world celebrate New Year's Day on January 1. Fireworks go off right at midnight.

People in Brazil get ready to jump over ocean waves.

In many **cultures**, people do things to bring good luck. People in Brazil often wear all white. Then they jump over seven ocean waves. They make a wish on each jump.

In Estonia, some people eat nine meals. They believe it will give them the strength of nine people in the year ahead.

Not everyone celebrates the new year on January 1. People in Iran mark it on the same day that spring begins. This holiday is called Nowruz. People clean their homes. They wear new clothes. It's time for a fresh start.

Many cultures in Asia look forward to the Lunar New Year. It's in January or February. Adults in China give children red envelopes with money inside. Firecrackers go off during colorful parades. *Bang!* The sound scares away evil.

A Lunar New Year parade in China

CELEBRATE YOUR COUNTRY

Are you proud of your country? Many have holidays to mark important days in their history. In the United States, July 4 is Independence Day. It's the day the country became free. Families and friends have picnics. Parades with floats go through town.

An Independence Day parade

A Bastille Day parade

People in France celebrate their country with Bastille Day. Soldiers march in a huge parade. At night, fireworks light up the sky.

HOLIDAYS THAT HELP US REMEMBER

Many cultures have holidays to honor loved ones who have died. In Mexico, they have Day of the Dead. People put up photos of those who are gone. They set out food and gifts for the spirits to enjoy. Many people dress up like skeletons.

Children dress up for Day of the Dead.

Carrying lanterns to the water for the end of Obon

People in Japan have Obon. They believe spirits of past family visit during this **festival**. When it's done, people place lanterns in the river. The lights guide the spirits back.

Other holidays honor people who died keeping their countries safe. In Australia and New Zealand, they have Anzac Day. It remembers those who died in war. People sing, pray, and read poems.

An Anzac Day event in Australia

Poppy flower wreaths made of paper

The United Kingdom has Remembrance Day. People place red flowers called poppies on graves of soldiers. During the day, everyone goes quiet for two minutes. This shows respect for soldiers who have given their lives.

HARVEST TIME

Are you thankful for food? Some people celebrate the **harvest**. In West Africa, there are many different yam festivals. In Ghana, a leader prays for the yams to grow. Then he takes a bite of one. Now everybody eats yams! People play music and dance.

A leader prays during a yam festival in Ghana.

Praying before the picked rice is put away

The rice harvest is a festival time in Indonesia. Before farmers put the rice away, people pray. They thank the rice goddess for a good harvest. They eat special rice dishes.

It doesn't matter where someone lives. It doesn't matter what religion they follow. There are many special things in life to celebrate. Holidays are times to remember that.

What holiday is next on your calendar? What will you do to make it special?

MAP

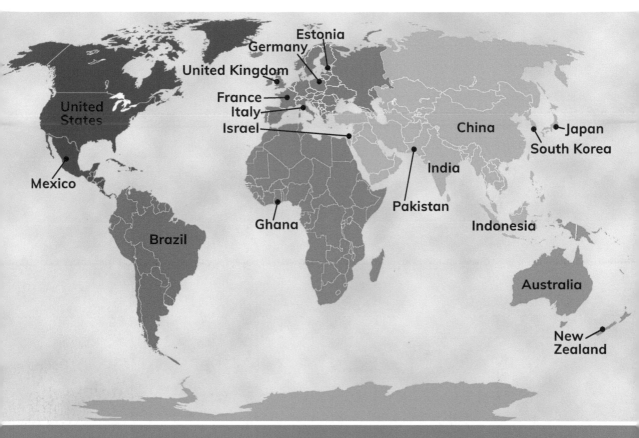

Around the world, people celebrate different holidays. See which places were talked about in this book!

GLOSSARY

Buddhist (BOO-dist)—a person who follows Buddhism, a religion based on the teachings of Buddha

celebrate (SEH-luh-brayt)—to do something for a special event

Christian (KRIS-chuhn)—a person who follows Christianity, a religion based on the teachings of Jesus

culture (KUHL-chur)—a group of people's way of life

custom (KUHS-tuhm)—a usual way of doing something in a place or for a group of people

decoration (dek-uh-RAY-shuhn)—a pretty, shiny, or colorful thing used to make something look nice

festival (FES-tuh-vuhl)—a time with special activities

harvest (HAR-vist)—a time when farmers pick and gather all the food they have grown

Hindu (HIN-doo)—a person who follows Hinduism, a religion that looks for truths about the meaning of life

Jewish (JOO-ish)—relating to Judaism, a religion based on belief in God and the holy book called the Torah

Muslim (MUHZ-luhm)—a person who follows Islam, a religion based on belief in one god called Allah and that Muhammad is his prophet

temple (TEM-puhl)—a building used for worship

READ MORE

Cho, Tina. *Korean Celebrations: Festivals, Holidays and Traditions*. North Clarendon, VT: Tuttle Publishing, 2019.

Grack, Rachel. *Ramadan*. Minneapolis: Bellwether Media, Inc., 2017.

Halford, Katy. *Celebrations Around the World*. New York: Dorling Kindersley, 2019.

INTERNET SITES

All About the Holidays
kcpt.pbslearningmedia.org/collection/holidays/

Spring Celebrations
kids.nationalgeographic.com/explore/celebrations/spring-celebrations/

Time to Celebrate!
www.timeforkids.com/k1/time-celebrate/

INDEX

Anzac Day, 24

Bastille Day, 21
Buddha's birthday, 14
Buddhists, 14

Christians, 6
Christmas, 6
cultures, 17, 18, 22
customs, 5

Day of the Dead, 22
decorations, 13
Diwali, 12

Eid al-Fitr, 10

festivals, 23, 26, 27
fireworks, 16, 18, 21
flowers, 13, 14, 25
food, 4, 9, 10, 14, 17, 22, 26, 27

gifts, 6, 10, 18, 22

harvests, 26, 27
Hindus, 12

Independence Day, 20

Jewish people, 8

lights, 7, 13, 23
luck, 17
Lunar New Year, 18

Muslims, 10

New Year's Day, 16
Nowruz, 18

Obon, 23

parades, 18, 20, 21
praying, 8, 10, 24, 26, 27

Ramadan, 10
religions, 5, 28
Remembrance Day, 25
Rosh Hashanah, 8

soldiers, 21, 24, 25